COURTNEY STONE

Unpacking the Fanny Pack

Fun facts and good vibes

This book was professionally typeset on Reedsy.
Find out more at reedsy.com

Contents

1

Introduction

Fanny packs, also known as waist packs or belt bags, are small, pouch-like bags worn around the waist or hips. These bags typically feature a secure strap or belt that fastens around the waist, allowing the pack to rest on the front, side, or back of the body. They're designed to be compact, lightweight, and convenient for carrying essentials while leaving the hands free.

Key Characteristics of Fanny Packs

- **Compact Size:** Fanny packs come in various sizes but are generally smaller compared to traditional backpacks or shoulder bags. This compactness allows for easy mobility and access to belongings.
- **Multiple Compartments:** They often contain multiple compartments or pockets, allowing for organized storage of items like keys, phones, wallets, sunglasses, and more.
- **Versatile Usage:** Originally designed for practical uses like carrying outdoor gear or sporting accessories, fanny packs have evolved into fashion accessories suitable for various

occasions and lifestyles

Evolution and History

Fanny packs have a diverse history, originating as functional accessories for outdoor activities and travel. They gained widespread popularity in the late 1980s and early 1990s, becoming a fashion trend embraced by hikers, tourists, and everyday individuals for their convenience.

Fashion Resurgence

While fanny packs experienced a decline in popularity for a period, they reemerged as fashion statements in the late 2010s, transcending their utilitarian roots to become stylish accessories. Designers, celebrities, and fashion influencers embraced fanny packs, elevating their status in the fashion world.

Contemporary Uses

Today, fanny packs are embraced across various demographics, from fashion enthusiasts to travelers, festival-goers, athletes, and individuals seeking a hands-free way to carry essentials. They're worn in diverse settings, from casual outings and outdoor activities to high-end fashion events.

Variety in Design

Fanny packs come in a myriad of designs, materials, and styles. From sleek leather designs to sporty nylon varieties and even high-fashion iterations from luxury brands, the diversity in fanny pack designs caters to different tastes and preferences.

Functional Appeal

The practicality of fanny packs lies in their hands-free convenience, allowing wearers to access their belongings swiftly without the hassle of carrying a larger bag. They're particularly favored in situations where mobility and accessibility are essential.

2

History of the Fanny Pack

Origins

- **Early Utility Bags:** The concept of a belt pouch or waist bag dates back to ancient times (up to 5000 years ago) when people used small bags or pouches attached to belts or waistbands to carry essentials like tools, coins, and medicinal herbs.

20th Century Emergence

- **1930s and 1940s:** Fanny packs, resembling the modern version, made their appearance in the US as military gear. Soldiers used small canvas or fabric pouches attached to their belts for carrying grenades, ammunition, and other supplies.
- **1960s and 1970s:** Outdoor enthusiasts and hikers adopted variations of fanny packs for their practicality in carrying items during hikes and outdoor activities. They were ini-

tially called "waist packs" or "hip sacks." Melba Stone, an Australian woman who wore a fanny pack regularly in the 1960s is in some circles considered the "mother" of the modern fanny pack.

Commercialization and Popularity Surge

- **1980s:** Fanny packs became commercially available, marketed as functional accessories for travelers and tourists. Their lightweight design and multiple compartments appealed to people looking for hands-free convenience while exploring.
- **Late 1980s and Early 1990s:** Fanny packs surged in popularity, becoming a cultural icon of the era. They were embraced as everyday accessories, worn by tourists, parents, and individuals seeking practicality.

Fashion Trend and Decline

- **Late 1990s:** Fanny packs began to lose favor in mainstream fashion as trends shifted towards larger shoulder bags and backpacks. They became associated with a dated or "uncool" aesthetic.
- **Early 2000s:** Fashion houses and designers moved away from promoting fanny packs, contributing to their decline in popularity in high-fashion circles.

Resurgence and Fashion Renaissance

- **Late 2010s:** Fanny packs experienced a revival in fashion, driven by a shift in fashion trends and a nostalgia for retro styles. Celebrities, influencers, and designers started showcasing fanny packs as chic and trendy accessories.
- **Inclusion in High Fashion:** Luxury brands introduced their versions of fanny packs, making them a sought-after item on runways and in high-end fashion circles.
- **Present Day:** Fanny packs have transcended their utilitarian roots to become versatile fashion statements. They're seen at music festivals, on fashion runways, and as part of everyday street wear. The diversity in designs, materials, and styles caters to a wide range of preferences.

3

Fanny Pack Types and Designs

Fanny packs come in various types and designs, catering to different tastes, functionalities, and fashion preferences. Here are some of the prominent types and designs:

Classic Fanny Packs

- **Basic Design:** These fanny packs feature a simple, traditional design with a main compartment and a zipper closure. They often have an adjustable waist strap and may include additional pockets for organization.
- **Materials:** Classic fanny packs are commonly made of cotton, nylon, canvas, or polyester, offering durability and water resistance for outdoor activities.

Fashion-forward Fanny Packs

- **Trendy Styles:** These fanny packs incorporate current fashion trends, featuring vibrant colors, unique patterns, and eye-catching designs. They might include embellishments like studs, sequins, or trendy prints, logos, and team symbols to make a fashion statement.

- **Luxury Brands:** High-end fashion houses offer designer fanny packs made from premium materials such as leather, suede, or exotic skins, elevating them into luxury fashion accessories.

Sporty and Performance-oriented Fanny Packs

- **Athletic Designs:** These fanny packs are tailored for sports and fitness activities, featuring lightweight and breathable materials. They often include features like reflective strips for visibility, moisture-wicking fabrics, and compartments designed for carrying water bottles or energy bars.
- **Running Belts:** Slimmer and streamlined, running belts provide a snug fit for carrying essentials during workouts or jogging.

Travel and Utility Fanny Packs

- **Travel-friendly Features:** These packs are designed with travel in mind, offering security features like hidden pockets, RFID blocking compartments for passports and cards, and durable, slash-resistant materials for added safety.
- **Convertible Designs:** Some utility fanny packs can convert into cross body bags or shoulder bags for versatility during travel.

Fashionably Functional Fanny Packs

- **Multi-functional Designs:** These fanny packs combine style and functionality, often featuring detachable straps or compartments that can be used separately as clutches or mini-bags.
- **Convertible Styles:** Some fashion-forward fanny packs offer adjustable straps or modular designs, allowing them to be worn in various ways, such as on the waist, across the chest, or as a sling bag.

Specialized Fanny Packs

- **Tech-Friendly Packs**: Fanny packs with compartments or features designed specifically for carrying smartphones, tablets, or other gadgets securely.
- **Medical or Utility Belts:** Customized fanny packs with specialized pockets or compartments for medical supplies or tools used by professionals like photographers, makeup artists, or medical personnel.

4

Fashion & Trends & Fanny Packs

Fanny packs have experienced a remarkable transformation in the world of fashion, evolving from functional accessories to stylish must-haves embraced by fashion enthusiasts and trendsetters.

The Pathway to Fashion Icon

- **Revival in Popularity:** Fanny packs, once considered outdated, made a notable comeback in fashion circles, becoming a statement piece in the late 2010s. Celebrities, influencers, and fashion icons began sporting fanny packs, showcasing their versatility and redefining them as chic and trendy accessories.
- **High-Fashion Acceptance:** Luxury fashion houses and designer brands incorporated fanny packs into their collections, elevating them from casual wear to high-fashion status. Fashion designers offered unique and luxurious interpretations of fanny packs, using premium materials, bold colors, intricate embellishments, and avant-garde

designs.

- **Casual wear Culture:** Fanny packs became a staple in casual wear fashion, blending functionality with urban style. They were embraced as part of everyday outfits, adding a contemporary and practical edge to casual wear from leisurewear and sporty ensembles to more sophisticated or eclectic styles.
- **Collaborations with Brands**: Many fashion brands collaborated with celebrities or artists to create limited-edition fanny packs, boosting their desirability and exclusivity. Fanny packs became a canvas for brands to showcase logos and iconic designs.
- **Social Media Impact:** Fashion influencers and bloggers played a pivotal role in popularizing fanny packs, showcasing creative ways to style them and influencing their followers. The aesthetically pleasing nature of fanny packs in photographs and social media posts helped propagate their fashion-forward image.

5

Functional Use of a Fanny Pack

Fanny packs, renowned for their practicality and convenience, offer a range of functional uses across various activities and lifestyles:

Travel Companion

- **Hands-Free Convenience**: Fanny packs offer easy access to essentials like passports, boarding passes, wallets, and travel documents while keeping hands free for other tasks.
- **Security and Safety:** Their close-to-body design provides added security, reducing the risk of theft or loss in crowded areas.
- **Organization:** Multiple compartments allow travelers to stay organized, keeping items like keys, headphones, sunglasses, and small snacks easily accessible.

Outdoor Adventures and Sports

- **Hiking and Camping:** Fanny packs serve as compact gear carriers, holding essentials such as maps, compasses, sunscreen, insect repellent, and small survival tools.
- **Running and Fitness:** Slimmer, lightweight fanny packs are ideal for runners, holding items like energy gels, phones, keys, and small water bottles during workouts.

Everyday Convenience

- **Errands and Shopping:** Fanny packs offer a practical solution for quick trips to the store, carrying wallets, shopping lists, phones, and keys without the need for a larger bag.
- **Dog Walking or Pet Care:** A fanny pack can hold dog treats, waste bags, keys, and a phone, leaving hands free to manage leashes or other pet-related tasks.

Concerts, Festivals, and Events

- **Security Compliance:** Many venues and events require clear bags or restrict backpacks, making fanny packs a compliant and practical choice for carrying essentials like tickets, IDs, and cash.
- **Comfort and Mobility:** Fanny packs are comfortable to wear for long hours, allowing people to enjoy events without the burden of a bulky bag.

Parenting and Childcare

- **On-the-Go Parenting:** Fanny packs offer parents a hands-free way to carry diapers, wipes, bottles, snacks, and other baby essentials while attending to their children's needs.
- **Family Outings:** Fanny packs provide a convenient way for parents to carry small toys, first aid supplies, and personal items while spending time with their children.

Medical or Specialized Uses

- **Medical Supplies:** Fanny packs can be adapted for carrying medical equipment, such as insulin pumps, allergy pens, or other essential medications, offering discreet and accessible storage.
- **Specialty Tools:** Professionals like photographers, makeup artists, or technicians find fanny packs useful for carrying specialized tools or equipment required for their work.

6

Fanny Packs in Pop Culture

Fanny packs have carved a notable place in pop culture, appearing in various forms of media and influencing fashion trends, music, films, and television shows. Here's how they've made their mark:

Film and Television

- **80s and 90s Icon:** Fanny packs gained widespread recognition during the 1980s and 1990s, often appearing in popular films and TV shows as a symbol of casual, everyday fashion.
- **Cultural Significance:** Characters in movies like "Clueless," "Home Alone," and TV shows such as "Full House" were seen wearing fanny packs, contributing to their association with the era's fashion trends.
- **Fanny Pack's featured in the 2000s:** In the 2000s, fanny packs might not have been as prominent in movies as they were in the '80s and '90s, but they still occasionally made appearances. Here are a few movies from that era where fanny packs were spotted:

1. The Hangover (2009): In this comedy film, characters Alan (played by Zach Galifianakis) and Stu (played by Ed Helms) wear fanny packs during their wild bachelor party adventures in Las Vegas.
2. Harold & Kumar Go to White Castle (2004): The character Kumar, played by Kal Penn, is seen wearing a fanny pack in some scenes as he and Harold embark on their quest for White Castle burgers.
3. Jackass: The Movie (2002): The members of the Jackass crew, known for their wild stunts, often sported eccentric outfits, including fanny packs, during their various pranks and stunts throughout the movie.

Music and Pop Icons

- **Musical References:** Several songs, especially from the 80s and 90s, made references to fanny packs, either in lyrics or through music videos. Artists like MC Hammer and Vanilla Ice were known for incorporating fanny packs into their performances and music videos. The Fanny Pack song by Bobby Bones and the Raging Idiots can be listened to on YouTube or Spotify.
- **Pop Icons and Fanny Packs:** Celebrities like Madonna and David Hasselhoff were photographed wearing fanny packs, contributing to their visibility and association with popular culture. More recently stars including Rihanna, Kendall Jenner, Fergie, Kim Kardashian, A$AP Rocky, Olivia Wild. Justin Bieber designed a limited-edition fanny pack for Tim Hortons called Tim Biebs which has been quite trendy in Canada.

Fashion Shows and Runways

- **Fashion's Revival:** Fanny packs have made appearances on fashion runways and in designer collections, repositioning them from outdated accessories to trendy and sought-after fashion statements.
- **High-Fashion Endorsement:** Top designers and luxury brands such as Gucci, Prada, Louis Vuitton featured fanny packs in their collections, adding a high-fashion appeal and cementing their place in contemporary fashion culture.

Social Media and Influencers

- **Influencer Impact:** Fashion influencers and celebrities played a crucial role in reviving the popularity of fanny packs. Their social media presence showcased innovative ways of styling fanny packs, making them appealing to a younger, fashion-conscious audience. The WWF personalities of the 80s and 90s were regularly seen sporting fanny packs. There is an Instagram page dedicated solely to WWF wrestlers and their fanny packs.
- **Hashtag Trends**: Hashtags like #FannyPack and #WaistBag on platforms like Instagram further fueled the resurgence of fanny packs, turning them into a trending fashion item. Fanny packs have become a versatile and stylish accessory in recent years! From their practicality during travel to their fashion-forward presence on runways, the #fannypack trend showcases their adaptability across lifestyles and tastes. Whether it's a sporty, sleek design or a high-end, luxury statement piece, fanny packs have made a remarkable comeback, redefining convenience and style. How do

you like to rock your fanny pack? #trendsetter. **If you like content that is 80% fanny packs and 100% positive vibes follow me on #fannypackvibes!**

Streetwear and Urban Culture

- **Street Style Symbol**: Fanny packs became an integral part of street wear fashion, embraced by urban communities and seen as an accessory that blended fashion with functionality.
- **Athleisure Influence:** The crossover between leisurewear and street wear contributed to the fanny pack's adoption among those seeking comfortable, yet stylish, everyday wear.

Cultural Revival and Nostalgia

- **Nostalgia Factor:** The resurgence of fanny packs tapped into a wave of nostalgia, appealing to individuals who remembered the accessory's heyday and saw it as a retro-chic addition to their wardrobes.
- **Cultural Icons and References:** From movies to music videos, fanny packs were seen as iconic symbols, contributing to their recognition and association with cultural references.

7

Choosing and Styling Fanny Packs

Choosing and styling fanny packs involves considering functionality, fashion preferences, and the occasion. Here's a guide to selecting and styling fanny packs:

Choosing the Right Fanny Pack:

Size and Capacity:

Consider the size needed based on what essentials you intend to carry. Smaller packs suit basic items. Avoid over stuffing a fanny pack, leave some wiggle room for finding items.

Material and Durability:

Opt for durable materials like nylon, canvas, leather, or water-resistant fabrics based on your usage and environmental conditions.

Design and Compartments:

Assess the number and types of compartments or pockets needed for organizing items like keys, phone, wallet, or travel documents.

Comfort and Fit:

Ensure the strap is adjustable and comfortable around your waist or hips, offering a snug fit without being too tight or loose. When in doubt choose a thicker wider waist strap to avoid twisting/rolling.

Purpose and Use:

Choose a style that aligns with the intended purpose, whether it's for travel, outdoor activities, fashion, theme celebration, holiday or daily use.

Styling Fanny Packs

Casual Wear:

- Pair a sporty or trendy fanny pack with jeans, joggers, or street wear-inspired outfits for a laid-back, casual look.
- Experiment with wearing it across the chest or over one shoulder for a modern twist.

Leisurewear and Fitness:

- Match a sleek, athletic fanny pack with active wear or leisurewear outfits for a functional yet stylish gym or workout look.
- Coordinate the colors or patterns of the fanny pack with your workout attire for a cohesive appearance.

Travel and Adventure:

- Opt for a practical yet stylish fanny pack when traveling. Wear it around the waist or across the body for added security.
- Coordinate it with your travel attire while ensuring easy access to essential items like passports, tickets, and currency.

Fashion-forward Statements:

- Experiment with high-end or designer fanny packs as a statement piece, pairing them with trendy clothing for a fashion-forward look.
- Contrast the fanny pack with your outfit to create a focal point or complement it with similar color tones.

Minimalist Elegance:

- Choose a sleek, minimalist fanny pack in neutral colors like black, brown, or tan to complement more formal or elegant attire.
- Wear it around the waist or slightly off-center for a sophisticated touch.

Mix and Match:

- Don't be afraid to mix and match textures, colors, and styles. Experiment with layering or accessorizing to create unique combinations.

Remember, styling a fanny pack is about personal expression and functionality. Embrace versatility and adaptability when choosing and styling your fanny pack to suit your lifestyle and fashion preferences.

8

Maintenance and Care of Fanny Packs

Fanny packs take a beating if they are living their best life. Beer, sweat, dust, campfire smoke. Maintaining and caring for your fanny pack ensures its longevity and keeps it looking its best. Here's a guide on how to properly care for different types of fanny packs:

General Care Tips

Read Manufacturer's Instructions:

Follow any specific care instructions provided by the manufacturer for your fanny pack.

Regular Cleaning:

- For most fabric fanny packs, use a damp cloth or sponge with mild soap to gently wipe the surface.
- For leather or suede fanny packs, use a specialized cleaner

or conditioner recommended for the specific material.

Avoid Harsh Chemicals:

- Refrain from using abrasive cleaners, solvents, or harsh chemicals as they can damage the material or color.

Drying and Storage:

- After cleaning, allow your fanny pack to air dry completely before storing it.
- Store it in a cool, dry place away from direct sunlight to prevent fading or damage to the material.

Material-Specific Care

Nylon and Polyester Fanny Packs:

- These materials are generally easy to clean. Use a mild detergent or soap with water for cleaning.
- For tougher stains, use a soft brush or toothbrush with gentle scrubbing.

Leather Fanny Packs:

- Use a specialized leather cleaner or conditioner recommended for the specific type of leather.
- Apply the cleaner or conditioner with a soft cloth and gently rub in a circular motion. Buff it dry with a clean cloth.

Suede Fanny Packs:

- Use a suede brush or eraser to gently remove surface dirt or stains.
- Avoid getting suede wet. Use a specialized suede cleaner if necessary and follow the manufacturer's instructions.

Water-resistant or Waterproof Packs:

- While these packs are more resistant to water, it's still advisable to wipe them dry if they get wet to prevent mildew or damage.

Special Care Considerations

Hardware and Zippers:

- Periodically check zippers, buckles, and seams for any signs of damage or wear. Lubricate zippers with a small amount of zipper lubricant if they start to stick.

Stain Removal:

- Promptly attend to stains by gently blotting with a clean cloth and mild soap or a stain remover suitable for the material.

Avoid Overstuffing:

- Avoid overloading your fanny pack with heavy or sharp objects that could damage the fabric or strain the seams.

Regular maintenance and proper care according to the specific material of your fanny pack will preserve its appearance and functionality, ensuring it remains a stylish and reliable accessory for a long time.

9

The Future of Fanny Packs

The future of fanny packs continues to evolve, blending innovation, sustainability, and functionality with fashion-forward designs. Fanny packs have proven the test of time. Here are some trends expected to shape the future of fanny packs:

Tech Integration:

Expect fanny packs to incorporate smart features, such as built-in charging ports, RFID-blocking compartments for added security, or integration with wearable technology like fitness trackers or smartwatches. Intergalatic planetary, planetary intergalatic.

Sustainability:

Some fanny packs are made from sustainable materials like recycled fabrics, organic cotton, or cruelty-free leather alternatives. Love to these companies. Seeking these small businesses. Lets vibe.

Modular and Convertible Designs:

Versatile fanny packs that can transform into different styles or be adapted for various uses, such as detachable compartments or interchangeable straps, will offer consumers more customization options.

Fashion/Marketing Collaborations:

Yes. Please! I volunteer to spread fanny pack vibes around the world through joy, love, dancing, laughter, travel, experiences.

Innovative Materials:

Experimentation with fabrics for durability, enhanced comfort, or self-cleaning textiles for easy maintenance could become prevalent.

Adaptation for Urban Lifestyles:

Fanny packs will continue to be embraced as urban essentials, with designs catering to the needs of city dwellers, such as anti-theft features, reflective elements for safety, or compact styles for convenience.

Customization and Personalization:

Brands might offer more options for customizing fanny packs, allowing consumers to personalize colors, add patches, or engrave initials, creating unique and personalized accessories.

Crossover with High Fashion:

Expect continued integration of fanny packs into high-fashion collections, pushing the boundaries of design and elevating them as statement pieces in luxury fashion.

Continued Popularity in Leisurewear:

Fanny packs will remain a staple in leisurewear fashion, evolving to adapt to changing trends and preferences within this style culture.

As consumer needs and preferences evolve, fanny packs are poised to transform further, blending style, technology, sustainability, and functionality to cater to a wide range of lifestyles and fashion sensibilities.

10

Final Thoughts

Fanny packs, in their evolution from practical utility to fashion statement, have showcased a remarkable timelessness that transcends trends and eras. Here are some final thoughts on their enduring appeal:

- The fanny pack's ability to adapt to diverse lifestyles, occasions, and fashion preferences underscores its versatility. Whether for travel, fitness, fashion, or everyday use, it remains a functional accessory.
- Its revival from a bygone era into a contemporary fashion staple speaks volumes about its ability to reinvent itself. The fanny packs journey from casual wear to high-fashion runways highlights its adaptability to evolving trends.
- The fundamental purpose of the fanny pack – offering hands-free convenience while carrying essentials – remains a driving force behind its continued popularity. The convenience it provides in various situations ensures its relevance.
- Beyond its functional role, the fanny pack holds cultural

significance. Its presence in pop culture, music, films, and its acceptance across different regions globally underline its impact and recognition.

- The fanny pack's ability to evoke nostalgia while seamlessly integrating into modern fashion illustrates its enduring charm. It bridges the gap between retro appeal and contemporary style.
- Fanny packs continue to adapt, embracing technological innovations, sustainable materials, and design advancements, ensuring their relevance in an ever-changing fashion landscape.

Conclusion:

Fanny packs have been and will continue to be the best choice for individuals seeking both style and convenience in carrying their essentials.

11

Bonus- The Hidden Pocket

Fanny pack gift theme ideas

- ***Baywatch Babe:*** Red swim trunks or One piece Red tank suit. Waterproof fanny pack. Fun shades and sunblock, whistle kidding, not kidding. Paddle that kayak, Lazy that River.
- ***Pickleball Baller:*** A runner's fanny pack which has a water bottle slot/holder. Instead of water bottle holds an extra pickleball or two. Inside pocket, neon sweat band and matching wrist bands.
- ***Van-life Vibes:*** Funky tie dye design or nature inspired. Inside the pouch: Gas gift cards, car air freshener.
- ***Happy Camper:*** Tent material, shiny nylon. Bug spray, sunscreen, flashlight, lighter, bear spray.
- ***Winter Wanderer:*** Fleece fanny pack for snowshoeing or skiing. Inside: hand warmers, chapstick, hot cocoa mix.
- ***Fresh Parent of the Month:*** The runner's fanny pack with water bottle holder, instead holds a baby bottle or sippy cup. Inside: small baby toy, pacifier, travel wipes.

- **_My Trendy Friendy:_** A designer fanny pack. That's one good friend! Inside: gift receipt.
- **_Cocktail Partier:_** Velvet or sequined. A fanny fit for a party! Inside: gum/mints, mini hairspray, money clip, lipstick.
- **_Golfer with Flair:_** Sporty, just the right size for a couple golf balls, tees and a ball marker. Iron or sew on a patch from their favorite golf course.
- **_Team Spirit:_** Your friend with the season tickets. Clear stadium guideline friendly fanny pack. Hand sanitizer. Face stickers with the team logo, cash for food/drinks.
- **_BINGO Buddy:_** How can you play 3 cards at once if there are purses taking up space on the table? Gift card for the establishment or cash and bingo dobber inside. Definitely pull tabs.
- **_Puppy time:_** Lots of W-A- L.-K's. So, a fanny pack is the perfect place to keep trainer treats, a clicker/whistle and poop bags at hand. So cute :)

Ready, Set, Fanny Pack, Word Find.

Three words will find YOU.

Pick at least one of them as your fanny pack activity to do today.

```
V  P  Y  T  W  A  L  K  U  F  H  I  K  E  R  F  C  H
G  Y  D  G  R  B  T  B  E  A  N  B  A  G  K  F  R  T
V  O  G  F  C  A  I  A  U  I  P  T  Y  R  U  N  U  R
X  Y  L  E  S  O  V  K  F  R  A  S  R  K  C  W  I  I
B  W  A  F  T  B  N  E  E  C  D  D  A  A  A  Y  S  P
E  G  J  R  A  A  O  C  L  X  D  O  S  I  I  Y  E  R
A  A  A  T  D  E  W  A  E  L  L  U  K  L  L  A  O
C  M  M  O  I  K  O  A  T  R  E  Y  R  U  I  K  F  K
H  E  X  U  U  L  R  R  Y  T  T  S  H  O  P  P  S  B
A  I  E  R  M  W  P  I  C  K  L  E  B  A  L  L  G  S
P  O  N  T  O  O  N  H  O  R  S  E  S  H  O  E  A  Z
S  D  A  N  C  E  G  C  A  M  P  F  P  L  A  Y  I  E
```

Peace and Love my Fanny Pack Friends!!

Positive vibes always :)

12

References

Fanny Pack (2023, September 11). In Wikipedia.
  https://en.wikipedia.org/wiki/Fanny_pack

OpenAI. (2023). ChatGPT (December version) [Fanny Pack Facts].
  https://chat.openai.com

Super Teacher Worksheets (2023). Retrieved from, Word Search Puzzle Generator
  https://superteacherworksheets.com

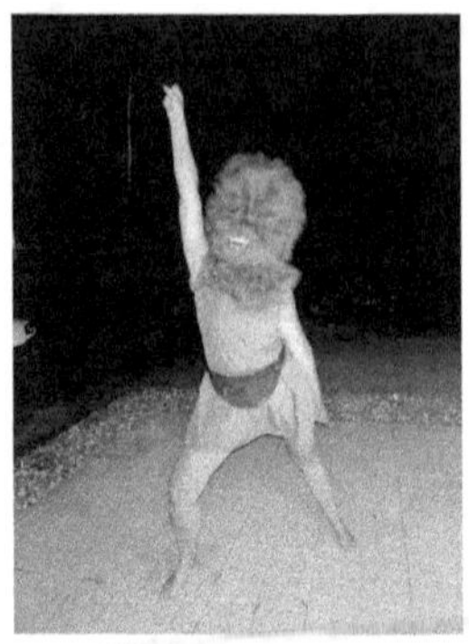

About the Author

My first fanny pack was in the late 80s. Neon embellishments for sure. In those days fanny packs were worn for special occasions like field trips, the State Fair, and summer camp.

In the late 90s my fanny packs were ditched for denim overalls, tiny backpack purses, messenger bags, totes, and clutches.

A diaper bag in my early thirties. And a baby front sling, and a baby backpack, and a wagon for that matter.

And poof. A decade or so later, I'm wearing a fanny pack again. Its carrying my golf balls and tees. It's a good look to with my new skirt from the pro shop. More golf please. More family, More freedom, More fun.

More fanny packs for: Trail walks. Kayaking.Pontoon rides. Sitting around the fire. Dancing. Frisbee.Snow shoeing. Camping. Portaging.Working on the short game. Throwing the football. Starry nights. Northern lights. Bingo Saturday. Traveling.Cruiser biking. Bean bags. Morning ocean walks. Sunsets.Sunrises. Dog walks. Airports.

To me fanny packs embody Freedom, Exploration, Movement, Favorite things and Favorite people.

I hope this little book brings a smile to everyone who reads it. Cheers my FP Friends!

instagram.com/fannypackvibes/